BOMB-SHELL PLUS

ACTION 911

Ed Kurtz

Published by
Westview Publishing, Inc.
8120 Sawyer Brown Road, Suite 107
Nashville, Tennessee 37221
www.westviewpublishing.com

SILK PURSE EDITORIAL SERVICES
P.O. Box 691
Tuxedo Park, New York 10987
editor@silkpurse.net

Cover design and layout: Laura Pelner McCarthy
Drawings: Kevin Martin

BOMB SHELL PLUS

CONTENTS

The Bald Eagle

Our great American eagle soars over the clouds and on occasion swoops down to see if the great American giant is still asleep. Finally the eagle notes that the great giant is coming to life. When the giant finally awakes, the eagle lets them see eye to eye.

Note the bald eagle flying majestically above . . . but DON'T LOOK UP!

THE OSTRICH

This is the ostrich. Why is this bird so unique? Although it might be mythical as he sticks his head, man, out of sight, one can talk to this bird face to face. The moral of the story is that at times we are stuck in a hole and cannot pay attention to the media, or newsreels, or our surroundings.

The information we get is that they report all events in Iraq or other nations. Report: one soldier was killed in Iraq, or how often the men go to the bathroom. Here in America, one person is killed every five minutes by an automobile, let alone those killed by tobacco or alcohol.

Withdraw your head. Gun control: Attention all criminals. On December 1st at 2 p.m. turn in all your guns. There will be no amnesty, nor coffee. All law enforcers will collect and record.

ATTACK ON THE WHITE HOUSE

This is the year of the attack on the White House, the year 2004, not BC or AD but AC. On a trip to the White House, I overheard one officer tell another that there will be an attack on the White House, or rather that his group will take back the White House. I think it would have been better to say the outhouse in back of the White House. This has been a daring plan for years. They must have accumulated many weapons. It is a big plan but the White House is well prepared and will "Bush-wack" any attackers. Warning to the demagogues: when attacking the White House, please be aware that there is also an outhouse. If that fails, proceed to Flushing, New York.

THE CRUCIFIXION OF PRESIDENT BUSH

The attacking force should attend church services and ask for Forgiveness, and say "ahmen." For all the bible buffs, the lightning will not strike, because he will have no lumber. Instead, he will be called the "burning bush. "

Pol-uh-ticks Explained

This has nothing to do with ticks that cause Lyme disease. Perhaps it is close. Here is something I am deeply concerned about. It seems that in elections, a few states have control over the nation. Why? Are they not part of the nation, or are they not "an-axed"? I believe that we should bring back the pins that claim "I am an American."

A fresh immigrant wanted to know why so many men are running for president.

These "can-the-dates" must exercise their right to play the American game because their grandparents did it in this sports way.

First, they gather in a group, which is called a crocus. This is a family that listens to the Democratic propaganda. This also includes a few states that make the decision of who they select to run against the president.

As for platforms, go back to "Gone with the Wind": Frankly, I don't give a damn. The politicians believe that they have a good platform. This could be true, but some platforms may have a trap door.

The fellow also asked why only a few states count. What happened to the other states? Thank goodness, the answer was simple. The other states have not been an-axed to the union. The whole bedlam is really organized confusion.

Now, it is important to organize a smart campaign. Go

down, Moses, and let our president go. I must reiterate, we have reached the dawn of civilization. When will the so-called American people wake up? We might understand sports, various games, but politics is one that is difficult to understand. Why the frenzy of running for office? As I mentioned before, we have reached an advanced "Ses-a-mess Street."

Who the hell said that this is the American way? The tele-buns are watching, and planning their next move, because we are telling them that they will strike as we predict it.

They are watching TV, listening to radio, what do they hear? That we want our president to step down, he does not know how to handle the country. Hot dog. See, America is all confused. So how can a country exist? We will help them get started. Hey, schlemiel, get the next bomb ready.

Warning colors are not understood by the person who is colorblind.

Elections are not a baseball game. These people stick to their team regardless of the consequences. Once a Democrat or Republican, we must vote for them. Not so. We can elect one not fit for that office. We must consider the problems aboard. While the dopes try to remove the President and call him names, the nuts in Europe are watching and think that our president is weak. Combine the Democrats and Republicans into one. They should be called Repo-dems. Have them sit together, make laws, and work as a unit.

If we throw away the bombshell, why not try the "nut shell"? To gain election, it is not necessary to have large sums of money, popular votes, stumping, speeches off the back of rail cars, kissing babies—ugh—shaking hands, silly speeches. Just get down to business and advertise on TV, radio, runners. Gossipers, hairdressers, barber shops, and the like.

Let each candidate express his platform, and the people will know who they should vote for. And the garbage cry, "I will vote for the party, no matter who."

Phoney-baloney. Silly debates. Find out the states that can elect a president. Just remember that there are fifty states. Do they count? Only buy the newspapers that are of your party . Get lots of money. A great push. Kiss babies, hug women, shake hands until fingers fall off. Knock the hell out of anyone that gets in your way. Or sing along with Mitch. Let's become mature. What's that? Advertise your position free on TV. Don't knock another candidate. And if you want to get elected, for pete's sake don't start goofing up by foul-mouthing the present leader.

They call the president all vicious names and want him to step down. Well, I have a simple system. Lay all the characters at the foot of the stairs, and let the president "step down."

The candidates go through the woods to create a stump. One does not cut them down to make a stump for the characters to sell their wares.

I propose a simple method to stifle these silly sessions.

Let the Dems and Repubs get together in one group where they can assist the president and help form a better union. Then we will call them the "Repo-Dems." Sit together and solve the problems of the country.

They take great interest in the polls. This is a great treat for the dogs. Don't forget the hydrants, too.

Every once in a while, the news tries to select the man on the street. I say, leave him alone. It's a cold day and he may have to relieve himself.

No president can solve the present day problems. Each time there is another problem, people will select a man for president who gives them fun and games.

As old Sharp-ton says, bring all the soldiers back. Great man, except that when the boys are back the only time we will have jobs is when they blow up a city. Boy, plenty of jobs. "Tis a far, far better thing I do now than I have ever done before." I would suggest that all these misguided people who hamper our president should crawl back into their burrow and come out to predict the weather.

Forget the war, bring back the troops. Now prepare to listen to the next bombing of our country when we relax. Remember Pearl Harbor. Our poor mother said, "I Didn't Raise My Son to be a Soldier." Well, my dear moms, we were not prepared for that attack. I hope we will be ready for the next one.

Amen (and some boys).

It's a Sad-dam Shame

Can you imagine if we did not take care of Sad-dam, and now other nations are getting on the bandwagon. Intellects say we can negotiate with these countries, poor souls. If we get a weak president, he can lead us in the pastures of cow manure, otherwise known as the "slippery slopes."

A great capture, but don't bring him here to America. Sooner or later our frenzy of lawyers will find him not guilty, because his father raped him at an early age. A good way to remember him is to stuff him and place him on the place where they tore down his statue. On the other hand, he is stuffed already.

Sleepers

You have all heard the term "sleepers." This is a group that lives in a country and when the time comes to do damage to that country, they are available. These people don't even take a cat nap. Are there people in this country that want the president to step down, and call him names? I think so. These are the politicians who want to take the present and gain power. One can hear and see them on TV every night. I am sick and tired of the "free screech."

We should separate this country into 25 states, have a great war, make peace. The enemy in other countries enjoys our stupid system called politics. The president should lock them up and I don't care if it's any hypes or pub-lick-ins.

THE WISE ONES

President Bush is fortunate to have media that could solve his problems. They interview the great men and ask them for their plans for our troops. Or they say now that the airlines have so much trouble perhaps the people won't want to fly. They can tell us how many more troops we need in Iraq.

President Bush would be wise to listen to the media, they can predict who will be the next president. Also know how many troops we need in the other countries, how long we can stand for the killing of our troops there, or who hit Nelly in the belly with a flounder.

People wondered why we have a senior "Stress-uh-me Street." Well, my dear, we have a "Stain-ur-me Street." It is called politics—great fun, although many are not laughing.

No matter how dumb an elected president would be, it won't matter as long as he is of the same clan.

Little fishie in the brook, papa catch them with a hook, momma fries them in a pan, and sister rides a bicycle.

THE PRESS

In the old days, we had the press to squash the grapes, or whatever we used to make wine or liquor.

The press of today presses the American public, and they are the gathers of "Bringing in the Shivs." This is a form of prisoners' knife that they hide in their clothing.

The press always mentions that the American people must know. Well, pressie buddy, the American people are still trying to find out what they should know. Some don't know which end is up.

They do an excellent job of reporting events very fast, but some of the papers lean towards opinions of their own. This does not go too well with people who are easily influenced.

It seems that the media is now able to advise the president on running the war, bring back the troops, why don't we have jobs, do take care of that, and the war will take care of itself. Ask questions, the generals will answer, ask them when the war will be over. Gosh, it's been going on for months now. How now brown cow. In the past, I assumed that the school children would learn of the nonsense that goes on in poli-ticks (oh, there's another one—pull it out).

Now the candidates are all lined up like the bowling game, with the ball facing them. Now the genius asks questions that they cannot answer, because they have not been inducted in the hall of flame. I was in service in World War II. Lots of bombing, dead people all around you. Watch it, here comes another one.

Aftermath: now we question and appraise each one. Like, did you notice the tense expression on his face? I wasn't sure that he really knew the question. These are the nine contestants. Remember that this is not a quiz show or some sports show. If elected, they will be in charge of a wonderful country, with foreign problems. We need a strong president that won't be led by foreign leaders. One big mistake and the bombs will fly.

Dear Collaborators, the enemy is waiting for a weak new president to be installed, one that will stop the war, bring back our troops, and later find out how far they will go before the bombs fall.

The Power of the Press. They can use this in the "Grapes of Rats." I found out the meaning of the "power of the pen" after one leaked in my pocket.

I am simply injecting the American spirit. We like comedy, so we will live with all the nonsense in selecting candidates with the usual fanfare. What is the cure?

What can we do? First, say after me: "Our Father." This might help. It seems that with the change of things as they are today, first we get women's suffrage, they are self-sufficient, not a good idea, we should hold women on a pedestal, but with their new freedom it's everyone for themselves.

The reason I can't run for president is that they might trace my ancestors back to Adam and Eve. Their son killed his brother. I am a Democrat but was born again. Now I want to be burped.

Ed Kurtz

GROUND ZERO, THE WORLD TRADE CENTER

SEPTEMBER 11, 2001

A VISIT FROM PRESIDENT BUSH

PHOTOS PROVIDED BY BILL COOKE

Ed Kurtz

THE BUILDING WAS STILL FALLING AS THIS WAS SHOT

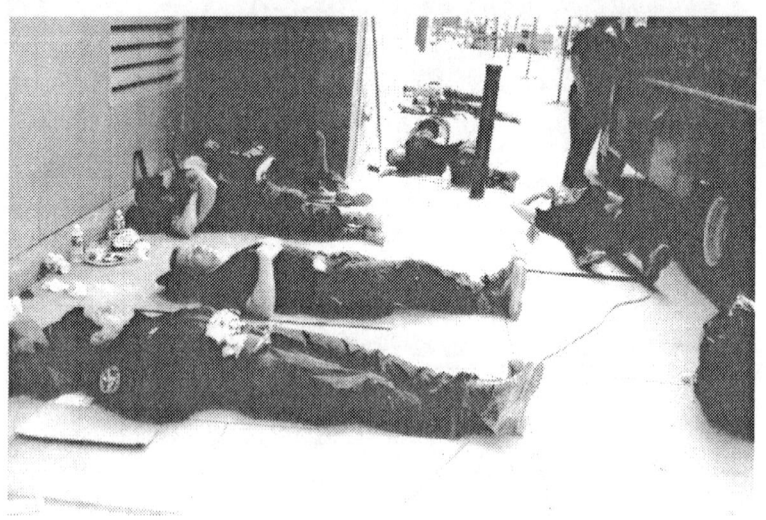

A SWAT TEAM RESTS

DIGGING FOR BODIES

THE SEARCH FOR SURVIVORS GOES ON

Ed Kurtz

WORLD WAR II

ED KURTZ DURING WWII

The United States Marines

I read that the United States Marines date from the founding of the Navy, and they are regarded as one of the most efficient bodies of men in the armed forces. On board ship, they perform sentry, orderly, and police duties. The Marines are sent first when a landing party is required or when help is asked by a United States war vessel by foreign countries. Candidates for enlistment as Marines must be between the ages of eighteen and thirty-five.

Well, my laddies, I was most impressed, so I decided to join. Big hero. We changed our clothes and had to get in formation. Here, facing us, was a loud-mouthed trainer. He finally arrived in front of me, and in a shrill voice asked me my name. I spoke in a voice just above a whisper. He said, "I don't hear you. This continued, and after a few sessions I yelled back, "WELL, BUDDY, WHY THE HELL DON'T YOU GET A HEARING AID?" Needless to say, my career as a Marine was kaput. The next Army will be the Salvation Army. Every Marine in the world will think that I am quite a brave fellow. Amen.

The Army

In World War II, I was in the Army Signal Corps. I wonder if people will think that "corps" is in reference to funerals. I went to five overseas countries. No yelling "Avast, ye landlubbers."

In the Forstmann Woolen Co., in Garfield, New Jersey, I enlisted in the Reserve Signal Corps. Here I remained on the job, and finally entered the Army Signal Corps, went to Camp Crowder, Mo., and completed basic training as a theory and code instructor.

We had to volunteer for the trip to England, our first stop. When we arrived in England we were given around 600 prisoners. Since our unit was waiting for further orders, we guarded them and they were quartered in warm quarters while we slept in tents with mud all around. We walked on planks to reach our tents. Veterans listening would say "T-S."

Cameras were not permitted, but we had at least a few photos of them. What was really funny was that we were given 40 prisoners to march to the train to do some work loading and unloading the cars. I was a sergeant, and the lieutenant called my name. "Sergeant Kurtz, here is the next 40." When the Germans heard that my name was Kurtz, all their ears were extended. Wow, they thought, we have a real buddy.

We had our company of experts. I was a high-speed code man, others were linemen, repair and installation men. After our unit came to England we did not remain together. They sent us to various headquarters but we later came together for a brief reunion.

Our complement contained all the necessary units, such as trucks, signal equipment, and everything that we shipped from America.

We boarded a boat with all our equipment and crossed the English Channel. When we arrived on the shore of France, we unloaded by climbing with full field pack down the rope ladders. We traveled in a train called a "forty and eight." Very few people know of this type of train. The forty designated that forty men could occupy one boxcar, and the eight meant that it could handle eight horses.

While on duty in five countries, some of the army boys were raising hell, but I simply went on trips as much as possible to enjoy all the wonderful sights.

LOCATION—BELGIUM

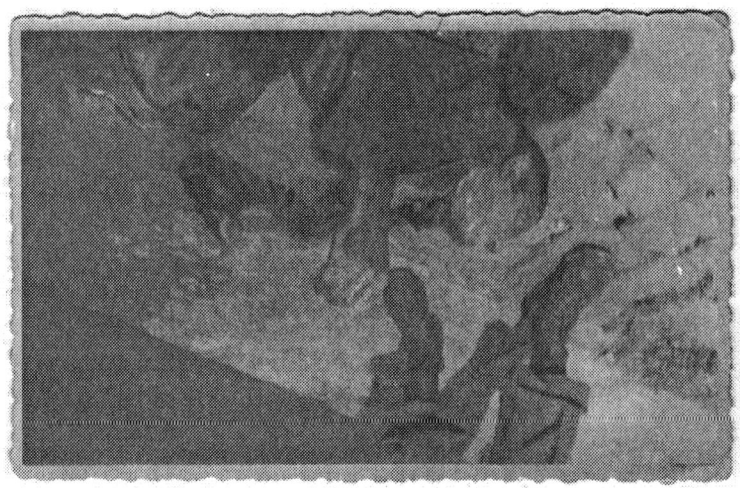

This incident happened along the River Muese, in Liege, Belgium. I noted that many Belgians carried a sort of suitcase. Wow, I thought, this indicated that these people were the top-notch officials. On contact, I found out that the suitcases carried fishing equipment and lunches.

Just under a bridge, a man was floating towards a few Belgians who were fishing. I asked one of the fishermen to let me use his fishing rod. As the floating man drew closer, I cast the fishing line out into the water, just over the man, and reeled him in. Naturally, he was dead. After being submerged for days, his body had produced gasses that brought him to the top.

Our Signal Corps men were stationed in Liege, and being a sergeant I told my corporal to bring out the Jeep and we headed out to Holland.

Now, you will notice me standing among the fallen. It so happened the four men were fished out of the German border. There were hundreds, who were sunburned and remained out in the winter snow until they were brought out. As you see, some of the men were badly wounded. You will note one of them has his head missing.

In the background were poppies and windmills. It's terribly sad to see the beauty of the landscape only to mar it with war.

JOCULARITY

Every war has a great character who keeps his or her sense of humor. You will recall that in Holland there was this lad who saved Holland from the great flood. In the wall was a hole, the lad put his finger into it and stopped the flood. I went to him and asked how things were going. He said he needed relief—so I took over the hole until he returned. Holy mackerel.

BACK TO THE RANCH (NAMELY THE MUESE RIVER)

The "buzz bombs" razed the city. The German planes did not do any precision bombing. Later, people pulled their children from the wreckage. This resulted in millions of deaths.

ENGLAND

FRANCE—OUR CAMP

BRIDGE BOMBED IN HOLLAND

OUR BOYS WITH BIG TOM CANNON

TELEPHONE OPERATORS

ONE OF OUR OPERATORS

When the war was winding down, since we were the Signal Corps, we established a telephone operation. We had more than twenty operators. Requisite: speak three languages, namely French, English, and Flemish. I was one of the non-com officers on one shift.

All our girls on the switchboard were from fine families. On occasion, some of our boys would visit the girls' homes and meet their parents. One lived on a very high hill. To get there we had to ride in a trolley, and it was like the

Toonerville Trolley in the funnies.

Paulette was about eighteen. Her mother was a speed typist and won competitions over women from other countries. The president of Belgium asked her to join the United Nations. Go, I told her, by all means. When the war was over and I was back home, she visited my wife and me and was pleased that I had advised her to go.

Of Paulette and her family, her mother and two brothers, I wonder how many are left.

When the war was over, we came home on ships, and arrived in our states—me in New Jersey—got off the train, and came home. No fanfare.

PAST TIMES

SCHOOL DAYS

I went to school in 1920, at the age of five. It was #5 school on Outwater Lane in Garfield, N.J. Although we had a sufficient amount of discipline at home, we objected to the type of discipline at school.

My first day at school was hazardous to my health. The teacher sat me down at a table with the other kids, who were playing with blocks and dolls. She assumed I would enjoy this part of the training, to which I strenuously objected. This was not my soda or whatever she was serving. The next ordeal was that she had the boys on one side and girls on the other side facing each other. While at this silly stance, we had to sing "How do you do my partner, how do you do today? We will dance in a circle. I will show you the way." No way. I had no use for girls to begin with. At home we ignored them, kids who associated with girls were sissies. She gave up and noted that I was incorrigible. In those days the teachers had full power, like the queens of old. Thank goodness none of us were ever beheaded.

As I grew older, my troubles escalated. We kids, naturally, enjoyed chewing all sorts of things. However, gum chewing was my downfall. Oh yes, we were adept at chewing bubble gum. All teachers had sight like a hawk in full swing after its prey. This one observed me chewing a mile a minute. Lines of apprehension appeared on my suntanned face. Contact was made. Ah-ha! She called me to the desk and with a talented sneer advised me of my rights and if I could not afford a lawyer I could have the principal. The further instructions were, "Now remove that substance from your foul mouth, place it on your nose, and leave it there until the cows come home."

I got one of my science books and found just what I was looking for: an eye for an eye. With great enthusiasm, I went to the candy store next to the school and purchased a material that you could chew. It had a sweet substance, and was great because, although it appeared like gum, it would not stick on my nose under these trying conditions.

The next day, I again sat in my chair, with complete confidence. Then, uh-oh—the teacher spotted me from her control tower, and she beckoned me to approach the landing field. "Well, my good man, what has thou of interest for me today?" That was pretty stupid; she knew darn well I was chewing gum. She started her well-trained procedures on command: place the gum on your nose, stand in front of the class, and present yourself as a stupid imbecile. With a sly grin, I knew she did not realize that she was accosting one of the young intellectuals, the "Master." Then, with a hideous grin, she said, "Place the gum on your nose." The moment of truth. "Dear Teacher, 'tis not gum that I was chewing, it is a wax composition that will not adhere to anything." "Ah so," she said. "Let's make a scientific experiment. Take the darn thing, put a curve in it, and place it over your nose, and hold your head up so that it will not fall off." Dearly beloved, my chewing days were over "toot-sweet."

Some of you old timers will get a kick out of remembering the young entrepreneurs who at the age of twelve were always seeking their fortune. There was an advertisement about selling a salve called "Rose-Bud Salve." This was used for cuts and bruises. The cost per container was 25 cents, and it had the appearance of a shoe-shine can. If you sold a certain amount, you would receive a gift. I sold enough to earn a telescope, two and a half feet long. After checking on the neighborhood's "aura," I knew that I was no dope cause I had the scope. This was to me a great treasure, and I would take it wherever I would go. Who knows, I might be called on to explain the celestial and heavenly bodies.

One day will live in infamy. I went to school with my telescope, climbed up on the windowsill, and scanned the heavenly orbits of the vast universe. All of a sudden, a fiendish hand reached out behind my neck and yanked me off the pedestal. It was none other than another teacher with physical prowess. A lecture, beyond human comprehension. She wrestled my telescope from my hands and said I would get it back at the end of the school term. I returned to my seat with an aura of disobedience. She will rue the day, I thought. She did not realize that my studies could culminate in a great study of the universe called "Celestial Phenomena." She had yet to discover that a kid of twelve could be so determined and dominant in his beliefs.

I worked very hard to earn the telescope, and I was going to prove that nothing could obliterate my intense attitude of science. Now the tide turneth. During that school term, I did not pay attention to any lecture or class participation. The proof of the pudding was that I was the only one in the entire school to receive a "minus zero" in my grades. The teacher was fortunate she did not report her findings to my father. He would have told her off, #@**% and four tenths. Suffer not ye little brats.

Regarding school days, it was a dangerous time for all of us kids. We gathered around the school grounds, where the "ring leaders" were active, and the lower echelon were following the roles of their leaders. Remember the spinning top? This unit consisted of winding a string around the top and pulling it, then letting go and the top would spin on the ground. Along came our fearless leaders (the creeps) and asked if we had a hole drilled into the top. If not, they would take away our tops. Sounds like the government. A day at a time.

Another gag was to have our leaders place a stick on our shoulders and stand back. This was to create a fight. With that, they would then say, "Three-six-nine, the fight is mine, I'll fight you any old time." This unholy tradition was terminated when my cousin, a large, strapping fellow who was in the Golden Gloves, intervened. Power is strength.

One day I was sitting in my classroom chair while a full-blown test was going on. Inadvertently, my eyes roamed around, across the aisle, to catch a few correct answers. Hearing footsteps behind me, I straightened up. I finally realized that this loving teacher was sneaking up on me. The teacher put a hand on each side of my head and slammed both hands together. This created an astounding clap of thunder. It was fortunate that the hands were not on my ears. I thought the Walls of Jericho had come tumbling down. This gesture could have created a hearing loss.

There are more stories from the torture chamber. If we, for some reason, went astray, we would have to hold out our hands, palms up, and the teacher would give us a few whacks with a ruler. Luckily, it was not a foot. If for some reason you went to the principal, he would ask you to bend over, and he applied a few paddles. And you would have to bend over, even if you name wasn't Ben Dover.

For the non-intellectuals, there was a pointed hat called the "dunce cap." This was presented to you and you sat in the fifth row, last seat. Another old trick was dipping the girls' hair in the ink well. For shame. If the school informed our patents of our misconduct, we would also be punished. Try these adventures for our misguided brats of today. It did not take too long to see "Edison" (that is, the light).

A good procedure was to require every student to read

aloud in front of the class some items presented by the teacher. For example, mine was "Fish Builds Brains." Well, I confronted the teacher, telling her and the class that I read an article in the paper that contested that statement, saying it was "not conclusive." She said, "Sit down." In another "sit down session" I read that the pirates were on an island. I told the teacher that the spelling was wrong, the "s" should be removed. Again the cry, "Sit down!" Another note to read was "Wind is air in motion," however there was no "Sit down!" I thought—it is better to air, but do it alone.

Now they talk about small school classes. Why? They say that small classes will promote better listening grades. No way. The real reason is that there is hardly any discipline, not like in our time. We had classes of 30 or more, and you could hear a pin drop. And attention was very simple: either you paid attention or got the ruler across the cupped fingers. No lawsuits. And if you got a couple of whacks, and your parents found out, you got another whack at home. This was called balancing the britches. (Remember Britches Bore-dough?)

JUDGES AND GANGSTERS

Imagine yourself sitting on the judge's bench and having to pass sentence on the surge of intellectuals who are never guilty. A plaintiff complained that a fellow stole some bottles of beer from him. The judge pondered for a moment and asked the number of beer bottles that the alleged criminal stole. With malice towards none, the man said about 15 bottles. "Well, my good man, 15 bottles of beer do not make a case." Case closed.

Then there was the fellow who the judge said to please approach the bench. Well, all hell broke loose when the fellow brought up a stool. Yes, the judge recovered.

Speaking of bootleggers, the reason they called them that was that they hid the booze bottles in their boots. When the cops noticed the fellow walking in a funny manner, they said "Boot up." No puss in boots.

Although the gangsters have almost disappeared, there are many intruders of all types—pickpockets, car-jackers, break-in and rape artists of all kinds. How about the car-jackers—why don't we hang them as they did for stealing a horse? Boy, that would stop it immediately.

Just watch the women in the shopping centers. They leave their bags in the carriages and continue shopping. To produce a "grand awakening" I tell them that they have a nice looking pocketbook. Lazy Mary, will you get up.

During the days of yore, or mob rule, as kids on our way to school all of a sudden we heard some rapid shots from a gun. In fact, it was a machine gun. There on one of the buildings was a man running for his life from roof to roof, while below was a gangster with a machine gun rapidly firing in an attempt to obliterate this pour soul. Yes, he got away, that time. Although gangsters were not masons, after the slaughter they put the victim's feet in a bucket of cement. Good for balance, and when they threw them into the Passaic River they swayed to and fro, while the fish swam by.

Some of the local citizens were quite ingenious. They had their stills in the basements, and above the roofs you could see some smoke emerging from the pigeon coops. In another means to conceal their precious stills, they dug tunnels under the house to ship out the products. Some of us kids did a good deed for our fathers. We went shopping in the fruit markets, where they gave us our bag of fruit and then bagged the pint bottle of booze. I suppose here we can call it "Fruit-Up." As one romantic bootlegger said to the girl, "I love your still."

We had a secret code or knock. If you wanted to enter the gin mill (saloon), you just knocked twice and asked for Gus. When our fathers were late coming home after work, we went to the gin mill and opened the swinging doors and yelled, "Is my father there?"

This was the "den of iniquity." Every gin mill supported a spittoon. This was a handsome receptacle placed on the floor at the foot of the bar, within range of the expectorant (plain spit). Those bar flies were like FBI men, straight shooters. It sounded like "ping." Ugh. On the men's room wall was a sign, "We aim to please, hope your aim is good."

On the border of East Paterson and Garfield existed a playground which was used for all types of sports. A short distance away was a hill called Cherry Hill. This area contained the proper sand for us kids to play with our trains, cars, and many other toys. On a clear and beautiful day, while thus playing, we heard the sound of a powerful car pulling up to the top of the hill. It contained Garfield's finest group of indigents, just peering at us and waving howdy. We waved back, and then they jumped out of their touring cars. Equipped with hand and machine guns, they just kept firing away, got back into their cars, waved bye, and rode off into the sunset. Wow. Here you see that these gangsters were in charge of the town. On occasion one could see while riding down Market Street a few good bodies lying along the road. Dead men tell no tales. Next time you get a hair cut, get a "crime wave."

The gang war was prevalent throughout the land. My brother had a green car, and as he stepped into the barber shop, he heard a gunshot and went out to see the reason. He found a bullet hole in his fender. They thought he was the enemy. After hearing that, I purchased a blue car. This episode took place around 1927. Nice time. As one guy said, can-sumption be done about it (Uh-cough, uh-cough).

Many alcoholics died from tainted liquor. I believe that

a good brain is a terrible thing to waste. That's if you have one. Now I smoke bacon and ham. I also drink orange juice.

THE FORSTMANN WOOLEN CO.

The Forstmann Woolen Company also included the Botany Mills in Passaic, N.J. They were instrumental in the betterment of the lives of thousands of people. Although none of our family worked in the Botany Co., we at times shared their problems. This company was employing many people who depended on their livelihood, especially after coming to America.

The Botany Worsted Mill was built in 1890, and the Forstmann Woolen Mills was built in 1902. They both settled in this area because of the city's abundant water supply, between the Passaic River and the Dundee Canal, and its proximity to New York.

Passaic industry developed later than most cities', when the immigration pattern had switched from mostly Irish and English immigrants to southern and eastern Europeans. The Slovak people joined the development of the city, and immigrants from Poland sent word back home that work was abundant. In the 1890s, Jews came from small towns in eastern Europe, where czarist dictators allowed them to live only in certain areas of the town.

By 1910, Passaic had become known as the "City of Immigrants," and by 1920, the Polish population totaled

17,000. Other nationalities included Ukrainians and Italians, but the largest group was from Austrian Galicia.

At the peak of production in 1918, 10,000 out of 21,000 workers in Passaic worked in the Botany and Forstmann plants. David Goldberg wrote about immigration labor at the turn of the century in his book called *A Tale of Three Cities*, namely Passaic, Clifton, and Garfield. "Work at the plants, where raw wool was processed into finished cloth, was long and oppressive. The raw wool was foul smelling and greasy, and workers often contacted anthrax, which came to be known as the 'wool-sorter's disease.'"

Women made up half of the work force in the plants, because the jobs did not require heavy lifting. Women split their time between raising families and working at the factory, working a special 8 p.m. to 6 a.m. shift.

A series of strikes in 1912 was followed by a year of long strikes by 20,000 workers, which paralyzed factories in Garfield, Clifton, and East Paterson.

Workers struck in 1926 because Botany and Forstmann had cut their pay and to protest long hours and poor working conditions. There was not much time for workers to be involved in anything other than raising a family and working long hours, and community life centered around the Catholic church.

The Forstmann Woolen Company had built about 30 company homes in Garfield, N.J., off Lanza Avenue. Only plant workers were permitted to rent these homes.

My two brothers and sister were employed at Forstmann in Garfield. I started at this plant in 1933, at the age of 18, as a machine oilier, keeping the machines at top running speeds. Between jobs, I was required to run errands for the office. If my hands were still oily, I took a paper and covered the mail. Lift that bail, tote that barge.

On one of these trips to the office, one of the main office managers asked me a question about something that he was interested in. I told him that I did not know the answer. With a stern voice, he told me that an apprentice should know many of these questions. He was taken aback when I told him that I was not an apprentice, and he said that I appeared to be a hard-working young man, and should enter the company's apprentice program. He told me to follow him to the plant manager's office. He introduced me to a man who asked me if I would be interested. I thanked him and wondered if I would get permission from my mother. He said that he had never head of a thing like that, but laughed and joked that if my mother approved, I could start on Monday. Incidentally, there was a long list in waiting for this apprentice program. (Before I get into trouble, I must mention my sister Mathilda, or Mitzie, and thank her for getting me the job in the first place.)

The apprentice program was a three-year term. The program was set up to make a six-month period in each of the woolen mill areas, then make an extra two years in the laboratory. Of the six months in each department, the fifth month was under the supervision of the boss. After the entire program, I was assigned to the wool spinning department. The training in the laboratory enabled me to understand all the types of materials used in the manufacture of wool.

By this time, the war was on and I enlisted in the Army Signal Corps and served my basic training at Camp Crowder, Mo.

When I returned from the war in Europe, my company manager introduced me to the president of the entire two plants of the Forstmann Woolen Company. The plant manager, my boss, mentioned that he would like to assign me to his staff and be a liaison between his department managers and himself.

The washhouse department was unique in its operation. The first step was to sort the wool into various phases, which was done by the wool sorters. My brother Louis was a supervisor there. The raw wool was then sent to the wool spinning department where it was washed and sent into a dryer. From there it went to the wool mixing department, where a mixture was made to the right color and quality. The wool was then sent to the carding department. Here the wool was sent through a series of rollers containing short wires on rolls which rotated around a large cylinder, and then finished by several flat rollers and wound onto rolls, which were then taken to the wool spinning department.

The raw wool was introduced into the hopper, which

emptied into long rectangular vats. These vats, in series, contained from 1500 to 2000 gallons. Wool cannot be pushed along by water pressure; instead it was moved by tines like the points of a fork. These tines moved in a long rectangular motion, which propelled the wool forward as it traveled to the next squeeze rollers. In the large vats was soap and soda to wash the wool While the soap did a good job, when there was a breakdown and the machine had to be stopped the soda would harm the wool. This system had been in place for about 50 years.

Not long after I was assigned to this department as quality control, and supervised all the wool, I spoke to the head of our laboratory, Mr. Wolf. A chemist in our lab investigated, and after various tests formulated a plan to use another type of detergent, without soda, and by golly, there was no more problem. The machine breakdown could wait. Unlike soda, which after washing left he wool flat, the new detergent puffed up the wool and permitted it to dry faster, thus the increasing production threefold.

All the plant's textile machinery came from Germany. Ten of our old carding machines became obsolete and the plant manager decided to purchase ten new carding machines for $800,000 from the Newport News shipyard. At that time they were building the *S.S. United States*. With two of my foremen, I visited the plant to investigate the progress. Well, sir, we were wined and dined by the president of that company for about a week. Since I was a supervisor of quality control, I planned the meetings at our plant with their supers and engineers to set up a so-called "shakedown cruise."

At Forstmann, I also set up the training program for new apprentices, who were required to complete a high school diploma and had to be eighteen years of age. I supervised their three year apprentice training. In fact, I was instrumental in designing the course.

When I noticed that some of these young men were top grade, I suggested that they look for other promising position. At least one went to West Point. When the course was completed after three years, their graduation was held at the Forstmann Library in Passaic.

The Forstmann Woolen Co. consisted of three main departments, the Garfield Woolen Division, the Weaving Department, and the Passaic Finishing Plant. My position as a quality control supervisor required me to ensure that he three divisions were up to standard in manufacturing the proper material for production.

Why did the textile mills close down? In the older days, you needed the warmth of woolen clothing, especially standing out in freezing weather waiting for a bus or walking to work. Later, with the advent of better transportation like buses and cars, the heavy clothing was not required.

After fifty years, the famous Forstmann Woolen Company, as well as Botany, finally closed its doors. You can imagine the thousands of people who were out of a job. My career was "ka-put." As president Roosevelt said, this was a day of infamy. I was only one of the few that remained at the plant when Stevens bought out our mill. I flew with some officials to various textile companies to try to revive our company, but no luck. After six months with Stevens, I tried to find other jobs. They said I was overqualified and so that was the end of the story. I later went into the painting business.

Back in 1920, mom used to say, "Bank the fire, turn down the kerosene lamp, fluff up the feather bed, and scoot off to bed." Adventure in the days of your, mine, or his.

THE MODERN WORLD

A Brazen Killer

Remember this: Pearl Harbor, the Main, the Alamo, and her birthday. All good shots, but there is another thing to remember: children, men, women are killed by the thousands. Families are devastated, many homes are broken, never to really recover. Just what am I talking about? Listen up.

This is no doubt a predominant killer with no remorse, which wanders through towns, cities, and states. He who hesitates is lost. Let's not linger and hope the situation will go away. We must forge ahead and bring this killer to justice. As President Roosevelt said, 'tis the "day of infamy." Forget the Alamo, and say "We have just begun to fight."

We must continue a relentless form of pursuit. Remember, this affects one and all of us. It is not a case where it only happens to others and never to us. Why me? We can predict a complete extermination if we form a more perfect union. 'Tis a far, far better thing I do today than I have ever done before.

We need a wake-up call, and awaken the sleeping giant. While we all agree that immediate attention must be afforded, just what is this terrible killer's name?

The automobile—just that simple.

There are 40,000 people killed by cars, probably more by tobacco and alcohol. Here is an opportunity to build a monument. They tell me this is different. Keep in mind that these deaths are not one shot, but every year.

Every time I go out to a trip nearby, and when I come home, my sister says "Wow, you made it."

The good old days?

Now, hitch up your horse, check the airless tires. Does the horse have to go, or will this be a roadway ceremony? Now you clomp along the unpaved streets or roads, get to your destination, hitch up the horse and do some shopping. How nice. Back home, you drive into the driveway, unhitch the animal, feed it, rub it down, and retire for the day or evening. Gosh, isn't that fun?

Those who have enjoyed the privilege of living at the beginning of the twentieth century have had the opportunity of seeing the transformation brought about by a change to a mechanical means of transportation—the auto, which has completely made over our business changes, social customs, and recreation activities.

Attention tin-lizzy cowboys (young whipper-snappers). In the old days, around the age of 19, way back then, without cars we used the buses, trains, and sometimes friends who had a horse and wagon. Other times, we just sat on the front porch and entertained the neighbors with our guitar and songs. Despite the inclement weather, we walked to school and business. Life was in the slow lane. What's the rush, it will be there for tomorrow. Movies—or "garlic houses," as they were called, because the kids had meals at home with garlic in them and thus had their own seats— cost 15 cents, or one could bring in a can of food to help the needy. As the girl from the Salvation Army said when some young fellow was promoting her, "We serve the needy, not the greedy."

THE AGE OF RAGE

There have been many ages: Ice Age, Stone Age, Iron Age, Coal Age, My Age. We humans have lived through all of this, but now, in 2004, we have met with the Age of Rage.

This is noticeable in our daily driving habits. They just can't wait. From a parking position they cut you off and get ahead. If you don't expect it a rear-end collision is very possible.

I tell people that I did a terrible thing last week. I stopped at a stop sign.

It is easy to get angry when people provide the so-called finger. If you ignore them it would be wise, but if you don't they become brainless and could do you much harm. Some people have been killed. What is very interesting is that whenever you encounter these people at meetings or jobs, they are mild and very friendly.

I am a member of the local "Crime Watch" program. We advise members to come to the meetings with a flat nose. This will indicate that they have their noses against the window pane, to be able to observe the violators in that area. The police attend these meetings and advise us of the various crime prevention materials available to ensure safety.

At one of the meetings, the police laughed because I said that I overheard one criminal say, "There's always a cop around when you don't want one."

One of the officers questioned a little old lady and asked her if she ever gave the culprit the finger. She said, "At every chance."

We also advise our group to restrain their tempers. Just make believe that you are sent to study their activities, as though a member of the "Morris Plains Home for the Poorly Wrapped Souls."

My nickname is 007 because I have a few inventions on crime prevention. On my car's rear bumper I have a 2-by-4 which contains many large spikes. Over this is a metal cover. The movement of this unit is controlled on the car's dashboard, and when the idiots blow their horns I slowly let down the unit until the bar touches the road. It usually makes sparks. If this is ignored, I simply let go—resulting in four flat tires.

Have a nice day.

While waiting for a light to change, the moron behind me was blasting his horn. I stepped out of my car, went over to him, and asked if he had to go to the hospital. He said no, so I said, "If you keep that up, you will have to go to the hospital."

Some years ago, a man in traffic waited for the light to change, while the man in the car behind him blew the horn incessantly. Well, the victim got out of his car, went over to the hornblower, lifted up the hood, and pulled out most of the wires. But, being a good citizen, he said "Have a nice day."

But road ragers, take heed: a friend of mine, who would become enraged because the red light did not change in time, within six months had a heart attack and hit another car. He died at the scene.

I hesitate to stop at a stop sign. I'm afraid that the moron in back is trying to take some gas while this frenzy is going on. I learned that the 25-mile speed limit was only used for parking.

The door openers just step out of the car and pay no attention to cars passing. One unlucky door-reemus had his door quickly removed, lock and key.

A scout friend of mine, Emil Orey, said that he was riding in a car when the bloke in back of them was blowing his brains out with his horn. Well, he gave him the pinky instead of the middle finger. I asked him why he did not give the man the middle finger, and he said he didn't deserve the middle one.

Observe the populace. They are going nutty. We see the violent nature in sports: hit him hard, that at least will break a few bones. Hockey was a gentleman's game, now it attracts a good number of hypos who knock each other around. Boxing is a great sport, if they still have a brain left to return to civilian life. Also the manner they play basketball. Hang on the basket. If we hung on the basket in the old days, we would have been a basket case.

If this obsession continues, there might be a real treat at the Meadowlands, like the lions eating the Christians. There would be thousands of applicants for miles around.

SOME SUGGESTIONS

A crime watcher: Every one of us can deter these Jolly Rogers, high-speed morons, from killing us or our children. We can use this unique method of slowing them down. In a small town, the police department could not afford any radar equipment, so they set up an ordinary hair dryer that they use in a beauty parlor, They just stuck it out of the police car window, and all the fools thought it was the real thing. Anyone for a permanent?

On the highway, if you get a flat tire and are speeding along, don't brake but step on the gas, because slowing down will pull your car into traffic.

When it's raining and the roads are wet, if you happen to go on the shoulder of the road and it's muddy, step on the gas and keep your car pulling ahead. If you brake, your car will swing off the road.

For example, I was traveling along Route 17 in New Jersey. It was wet, and a car ahead of me wandered off onto the wet and muddy side of the road. He tried to get back onto the road when all of a sudden he hit a tree. I was in back of him, he then pulled over parallel with me, and we both went down into the side ditch. He locked with my car, so I had to get out on the passenger side. But trying to open his driver's side door was impossible. I told one of the other car divers to get help, bring along a crowbar so I can force the door open. We finally opened the door. His both hands were on the wheel, and I had to pry each finger loose. The doctor arrived and gave him an injection, but the driver died. His wife had a hole in her head, while the rear passenger had a broken leg. The state trooper asked the gathered group if they saw the accident. One from New York was a witness. The next day, a police inspector came to the house and asked me what I suggested for future safety. I told him to remove the center trees, which they did.

SOME OTHER SUGGESTIONS

FBI. When you capture a criminal, and he is in and around a car, don't waste your time shooting back and forth. Send in a controlled small unit, equip it with a bomb, and clean up the mess. Another way: set up a sharpshooter in a higher building and they won't know what hit them. Why should we lose men like the FBI?

FBI could also mean Full-Blooded Italians, Full-Blooded Indians, Full-Blooded Immigrants

For a police chase: Let a helicopter drop a large round, tough blanket right on top of the fleeing car. Bam! This is called a "blanket policy."

When a police officer pulls over a car for questioning, let him put a unit in front of the guy's back tire, and if he tries to get away, the tire will explode. Harmless, but it will stop the car.

Safety on our planes: all seated passengers should sit in their seats, with the seatbelt strapped and made of material that cannot be cut. The passengers cannot get out of them unless relief is needed. The air marshals can lead them to the rest room. On long trips, the marshals can have two or three do some deep-knee bends while they hold a pistol to their heads. However, if they subdue a criminal, just open the door and let him go.

Plane mishaps: At rare times, some of the wheels on landing will not lower for a safe landing. Each plane should be fitted with smaller safety wheels that can also retract. There is great danger when a plane lands not on the wheels but a belly landing. The body of the plane scrapes along the ground and could cause a fire or explosion.

NASA tests for a trial in space, so they sent Manny, Moe, and Jack with a monkey. All went fairly well until the trio became very bored, so they radioed NASA. "Orbiter calling NASA. The monkey is working all the controls. What shall we do?" The great answer from NASA was, "Feed the monkey!" That sure was an ass-troo-nomic answer.

Adew. Innocent enough, but enough of the drops can create havoc, like drowning the populace.

AT THE SUPERMARKET

Let's go to the supermarket. The women are looking for their carriages. I calm them down by saying that each day will always have a missed-carriage.

Heavy traffic in and out of the lanes. Watch it, there goes another cell phone. Running into boxes, carriages, people.

Naturally, I cannot cope with the mob. They stand in line and are ready to go home. How can I wait so long?

I was waiting in line at a supermarket when the fellow in front of me was ready to leap out of his skin because there were eight people in front of him.

"Say, chum, let's get out of this line," I said. "I also can't stand these stupid lines."

"Where should we go?" he asked

"We'll go home and put on our hunting clothes. Take along a bag. We'll go hunting and then we'll bring home the game. Your wife can skin it. We can also go to a vegetable garden and pick up some veggies."

Like a bolt of thunder, he shut up and waited quietly from then on.

I have been a scoutmaster since 1940, and now, in 2004, I make it my way of showing people some magic when they are in line, to make their day easier, and they begin to laugh. When I make some girls laugh, they say "You made my day." I then ask, "How about the evening?" They politely say, "Get lost."

I have a sign on the back of my sweater—"available "

Here's a little trick: tie a bag around the handle of your carriage. That way you will always know which carriage is yours. When parking at a food market, on the back of your shopping list mark the number of the line that you parked in—no sweat. Keep spare keys in your pocketbook or purse. Wrap them so they won't fall out.

When you leave your house, put a strip of Scotch tape on the part where the door opens. If gone, call 911.

THE PASSAIC AVENUE INCIDENT

Clifton, New Jersey. Time to trim the hedges. A brave soul, I gathered my equipment, which consisted of a mere hedge cutter, affixed the cord, and began fanning the cutter in a sweeping motion. For the time being, all went well, until oops! the cord got in the way of my swatches and pow! the cord was severed. Don't go away, because this cut line also activated a fuse to blow in the main fuse box, and who knows where it disconnected the current line. Behold.

Here on Passaic Avenue, near the cemetery, I live happily with my cocker spaniel, who acts a good friend as well as a fine watchdog, with only a few accidents along the way. All else is very quiet.

The front porch is encased in glass, which gives me a view of the New York skyline. What better place to enjoy my solitude than this place. Enough, onward with the story. Linger now.

Except for a few night calls by some birds and an occasional horn-blowing idiot, all seems peaceful. But I spoke too soon.

Around two in the morning, my faithful guard erupted into a fierce bark. This was accompanied by his continuous running from the rear inside door to the front porch. I slid out of bed and reached for my trusty revolver.

I entered the porch, only to note that a young lady was attempting to enter the porch. She was screaming and banging on the door and yelling for me to let her in. Remember, the fuse had cut the light off on the porch, so all I could see was her blurred figure. Being a good "crime watcher," I was reluctant to let her in.

The next best thing is to call 911, and in a flurry the police were there, coming up the steps. One officer, in a semi-shocked voice said, "By gosh, she is absolutely naked." Quickly he applied his coat to cover her figure, and as I bravely stepped out of my domain the officer called my attention to all her clothes that were strewn about on the lower landing of the steps.

She told the office in a quivering voice that she had met two men at one of the bars in Passaic (although any bar could be barbaric), and they were so nice, and when they offered to drive her home they passed many houses and since she did not acknowledge their good intentions, she was tossed out bodily after they disrobed her. All she wanted to do was to go home and rest. Her story was that they had a good time at the bar, and who would ever think that they were of that type, but it did not turn out that way. She cried bitterly and had learned her lesson and would tell her friends to be on the alert for these really nice fellows.

These true stories happen all across the country. There is rape, murder, kidnapping, and an assortment of foul plays. A lesson learned is a lesson earned. Take care.

Ed Kurtz

SCOUTING

ED KURTZ ON SCOUT PATROL

I have been involved in scouting for more than sixty years.

One day we were at a "Show-and-Do," where various troops show their stuff, a very interesting display of bridge building, setting up tents, and many other items where the troops can learn and take the knowledge home.

On this sunny noon, my friend—who had about the same time in scouting as I did, about 65 years—and I were talking about having wimmin join our troop. Along came a beautiful young woman and asked us if she could join and talk about scouting. She then pointed to several wimmin, and said there is a scoutmaster, another girl was a scout assistant, what did we old timers think about that?

Like the old codgers that we both were, I spoke up first. I said, "I think that's great."

""My goodness," she said. "Really?"

I said, "Sure. Now we don't have to sit alone when the boys go hiking."

Here was another fragment of a bombshell. In a huff and a puff, she took off like a jackrabbit.

Explanation: While the wimmin are a great help to scouting, I don't want any wimmin mixed up in our troop. Now the do-gooders will rant and rage, but a boy looks up to a man, so what have these gals to offer?

Ah-men, and some women.

Keep the Scout oath. The udder ones go berry pickin'.

When I had 26 Scouts in Saddle Brook, they called me "the Gestapo." I agree. When I told boys to jump, they asked me how high—and did not come down until told.

One of my scouts said. "It's cool." I immediately gave him a sweater.

Another one said, "Mr. Kurtz, show Joe how you can

disappear."

"Well, Joe, close your eyes." You think I can really disappear?

The scouts must do a good deed. Every day you heard you should help the old lady across cross the street. Even if she did not want to go, a Boy Scout insisted.

As a scoutmaster I, too, tried to help an old lady across the street. She put up a grand fight and hit me with her pocketbook. No more crossings.

In the deep woods, how do we start a fire? Well, we rub two scouts together.

Get lost only if someone tells you to. Getting lost in the woods can be avoided. Take along an area road map, note where you went into the woods. On the map you will note that it shows the entire area where you will enter. As you enter the deep woods, it will be easy to box yourself in that area. If you do not have a compass or the forest trees are too tall to note the shadow, to tell direction take a toothpick or a small tree and hold it vertically over your fingernail, and you will note the shadow on your nail.

SERPENTINE TALE: A TRUE STORY

As a young man, I was always interested in hiking and camping. Lake Mombasha, situated across the New Jersey border in New York, is a large lake, surrounded by majestic forests and visited by many.

On one of my trips along the Appalachian Trail, which runs through the New York area, well up in the higher portion of the mountain, there were large flat rocks on some area of the trail.

As a scoutmaster, I have spent many years in the woods and the along trails, which made me alert to my surrounding area. Now here I am, hiking along an uphill trail, and I note that the large flat rocks that comprise the trail have some leaves gathered in a bunch. Ah-ha! There under the leaves is an area exposed enough to reveal a copperhead snake (not very large, probably less than four feet).

This is an example of what can happen to the unwary when going up a trail. Some inexperienced hikers have even encountered a venomous snake. Carry a long tick, sturdy enough and about six feet in length. With this pole you can flush the trail and note if there are any snakes in the bush.

But if you try to pin the snake down with either a straight stick or a forked stick, the rock under the snake will not hold the snake and it will crawl right through, so here's the trick. Cut a straight stick or use the one you use on the trail, and also a forked stick. Pin the snake down with the straight stick and when the snake rears its head, you can try using also the forked stick.

After I caught the snake, I took a string from my pocket and formed a noose, lowered it around the snake's head, and tied its body to the stick. "Jungle Jim" with this trophy, I entered the small town and was received as a hero.

Back in 1940, I had 35 boys in Troop 112. This was a tough gang. While going to the scout meetings. some of the local yokels, the wise kids, called our scouts "chippy shooters." That's all our boys needed—we roughed up a few and the episode never happened again.

People have the wrong impressions of scouts and their activities. For example, one of my friends said, "They're a bunch of sissies, running around with shorts and neckerchiefs." Well, fine, but I showed him the scout magazine which illustrated some scouts skinning a rattlesnake and cooking it. (Boy, let me have some more.)

At one of our parties a young man said that he was fearless, and that no animal could scare him. He said this just to annoy me, so I invited him on one of my trips onto the top of one of our mountains. This was a weekend trip, which would give me ample time to test his mettle.

Time elapsed. There we were, just the two of us, and around the time it was beginning to get dark I left him by the campfire and went behind a large boulder to observe his brave attitude. It was not too long before the first wave cry of, "Hey Ed, where are you?" Later, with more crescendo, he exhibited the natural fear of the unknown, yelling, "Hey Ed, don't leave me alone!" What is very interesting, as woodsmen know, is that the shadows create animal-like creatures that can make a small pine tree look like a bear.

In one of my hikes, I set my pup tent right on a deer trail and during the early hours a large deer stopped in front of my tent and snorted. I simply banged a few things in the tent, and he went away. Deer me.

About 12 boys applied for membership in Troop 4, at the Sacred Heart Church in Clifton. I lined up the boys, and as a former Signal Corps sergeant, I thought I would try a few tricks on the "greenies." I stood at attention, and yelled real loud, "Fall in!" Well, wouldn't you know, they looked at the floor, and thought I meant fall in the hole. I told them not to fear. "At the next meeting, when I yell 'jump,' don't come down until I give the orders!" Tumultuous laughter rent the air.

SERVICE PLUS

Let Ron Gorun describe our "Service Plus" group of about 25 men :

We have a group in our scouting in Passaic County called "Service Plus." There are a few requirements, so that one may not join just for the name. We afford all types of assistance to the cub scouts and other scouters. We keep in touch, meeting with the top scout brass and ironing out important matters.

May the light shine on you, with good batteries. God bless.

JOHN "CHIEF" KRAMER

John Kramer, also known as the Chief, was almost a lifelong scout and scouter, one of those persons who are rare and valuable like a jewel.

As a youngster he was a Boy Scout, and eventually attained the rank of Eagle. He continued his affiliation with the scouting program in the his hometown as a volunteer scouter. He served on the troop committee and worked closely with the boys. As he matured, he began to expand his service in scouting by serving with the council Adult Training Program for scoutmasters and committee members of local units. As the neighborhood commissioner, he served the troops in Garfield, N.J.

John received the Silver Beaver, the highest award of recognition for service to the community and the scouting program by an adult volunteer in the program.

John found time to help the rangers at the council Camp Aheka for many years. He was one of the founders of the special volunteer group called the Service Plus. This group's purpose was to help scouting by helping working programs. To belong to this group, the volunteer must have completed scoutmasters and adult committee training.

John's nickname "Chief" was a result of his annual visit to the Indian camp in Maine. He became friendly with the Indian chief and he was asked by the chief to join the tribe. The story is that John was afraid the chief had in mind for John to marry his daughter, so he never returned to the camp.

John "Chief" Kramer continued to be the Chief for many years, providing service for the boys and the leaders. Upon his death, a testimonial service was held, with many scouters in attendance. He is missed, but remembered.

—a remembrance by John Sloan

JOHN SLOAN

John Sloan has a long career in scouting. He can be seen at any one time in every troop in the New Jersey reservations. John was very instrumental in organizing the special group of scouters called Service Plus.

When we went camping with some of the men, John said that each one as they enter the group shall be watched as to their activities around the camp. For example, I was called "Dit-Dah" because of my affiliation with the Signal Corps.

At one time John and I and John Kramer traveled to every scout camp in New Jersey. As we drove around wearing our broad-brimmed scouting hats other passengar cars slowed down, because they thought we were state troopers.

John was instrumental in training new scoutmasters. He would start them on a forest trail and they would study the map, and if they arrived at the proper destinationt hey would be treated to a fine dinner in the forest.

John moved to Virginia and still worked with the local churches to help train scouters. The Silver Beaver award was given to the three of us. To get this award, a scouter must serve ten years. John Kramer, John Sloan, and I each served for some 60 years.

THE TWO FACES OF SNAPPER

EMIL OREY

Emil "Snapper" Orey is the man who built a castle around scouting. He is a great friend, and a leading factor in keeping the Service Plus group together. Here's how he lists his many titles:

Scoutmaster, Cubmaster, Silver Beaver recipient, District Award of Merit recipient, Chief Cook but not Bottlewasher, Committee Chairman, Camporee Chairman, Arranger of Service Plus Overnights, Chief Rain Cloud (reputation earned because of many, many, many rainy overnights), Internal Revenue Dues Collector, Delinquent Secretary of Service Plus, Latrine Orderly, Top Banana . . .

Amateur Radio:
Why You Should Become a Ham (No Eggs)

Why should you become a ham? There is a very simple answer. As you progress in your adventures, you will with moderate equipment be in a position to contact over 325 countries.

To become a ham, which is a radio operator with the proper license, is to enter a world of mystery and adventure. You will have a handheld radio similar to police radios. You can use this radio on field trips and car travels, and you will be in the much needed communications for safety and plain fun as you meet thousands of fellow hams ready to serve you in your needs.

First, by all means attend join a local ham radio club. Here they will instruct you in the procedure of getting a ham ticket. If there is a radio ham in your vicinity, call on him and he will code you in the right direction.

The stages of ham operating are:
Novice
Technician
General
Advanced
Amateur Extra

Getting started is not a hassle, you can obtain ham radio sets from hamfests, where hams gather to buy new or used equipment. Here is an easy way to meet hundreds of hams.

In the early 1900s, short wave radio was introduced on some ships, when before they had to rely on communication with flags and sight signals.

For the first time, this ship was hit by another ship. The radio operator on duty, and his quick action under trying conditions, saved many of the hysterical passengers. It was a great moment for this young boy, especially the great reception on landing. Soon it was introduced to all ships.

By now we all have learned the frightful journey of the Titanic.

When the ship ran afoul of the iceberg and flew flags of distress, a passing ship thought they were having a celebration went on. An important factor few people realize is that the radio operator could have saved all these lives if the captain had not been so lax. Since the ship was so great, so "unsinkable," the radio operator used the radio only to contact friends of the passengers at home. In fact, he was asleep just before the ship hit the iceberg.

I believe that radio operators are unsung heroes. Countless ships sending the famous "SOS" have been contacted by our radiomen, who then pass the information to the Coast Guard. During hurricanes, floods, typhoons, and many other incidents, the radio operators come through, and they never receive any pay for their services, nor would they accept any.

HUMOR

A Cry in the Wilderness

Let's journey to the land of the Pilgrims, as in "Pilgrim's Progress." So it came to pass, but not like in football, that this story unfolds by the shores of "Kitch-e-goomy." This is a lakefront property. Without ado, we find Captain Miles Standish inspecting the landscape. You will recall Priscilla Mullins and John Alden in a love affair to which is attributed the famous saying "Speak for yourself, John."

On one of his field trips while Standish walked along the shores inspecting the area, he heard an uproarious laughter. He stood fast, and lo and behold, coming up the trail was our Princess, "Minne-ha-ha." She became hysterical and during her laughing spree was slapping her buckskin thighs and proliferated with laughter.

Standish, a very stern man, motioned her to stop this stupid behavior, which was unbefitting a young princess. "Why are you laughing," he said, "when all around you exists this pestilence and lack of food, which cannot be ignored?"

Her answer was, "I am laughing because I have Delta

Dentals."

He said, "Boy, that's a mouthful."

The adage of "tongue in cheek": remember the dentures.

Brilliancy personified: Attention, all walks of life. Take a bus.

The Singer Sewing Machine Company can use this slogan: "Wishing won't make it sew."

For the oiling companies: "Tools get rust."

I was born and bread. And liked it with butter and jelly.

One day I was filling out a medical form. I filled out height, weight, eyes, hair, and noticed it read "Sex." By golly, I wrote, "Not too often."

After a brief exam, the doctor said that all systems were go, but one thing he was not quite sure of. Finally he said it seems as though I had been removed from breast feeding too soon. I asked him, Can I now make amends?

Another problem: I asked the doctor if I could be born again. His fast answer, "Too big."

A CHRISTMAS LETTER FROM OUR FRIEND BARBARA ROONEY

CHRISTIAN ROONEY

Whoever said life begins at 60 sure knew what he was talking about, because I can tell you it's no picnic being 6! I know, I know . . . this is supposed to be a cheerful Holiday Letter but bear with me, it's been a very tough year for yours truly.

As you all know by now, Christmas is always a big deal around here and last year was no different. We had a great Christmas celebration was Babcia, Dziadzia, and our friends. It was made that much more special by the amazing snowfall we had that day . . . it was truly a Winter Wonderland.

It was just after that, however, that the bottom dropped out for me. Two days after Christmas, my Dziadzia passed away. It was a huge loss for me and a very sad time for our family. We buried him on New Year's Eve Day and spent a quiet evening with friends that night. Things have never really been quite the same since he's been gone.

Everyone was very supportive throughout the year and slowly, with the passage of time, things got a little better. I was wrapping up my last year at Bright Horizons so it was a time of last hurrahs with my friends. We had parties, went to the movies, and I finally got inside that Medieval Castle.

We stayed close to home most of the year, making trips to the beach whenever we could. It was the first time I really got to enjoy the boardwalk, since I'm tall enough now for most of the games. Another first this year was gong to see the circus with my "brothers" . . . it was spectacular.

Summer seemed to come and go quickly and before I knew it, I was being fitted for my school uniform. I was very excited to finally be going to a "real" school with my "brothers." Little did I know what was waiting for me. What I thought was going to be a great time turned into endless hours of sitting in a classroom learning lessons then going home to do homework. Babcia was away for almost two months, so Mom and I had a really tough schedule. It didn't help that my teacher kept sending Mommy notes about my behavior. After that, things started disappearing about here . . . like my toys. TV viewing was cut back quite a bit too . . . I can imagine what I missed! I really wish I could go to Hogwards with Harry Potter . . . things always seem to be much more exciting at his school!

When Babcia got back, things eased up enough so that I could finally start my karate classes (courtesy of Uncle Bruce). It's been a couple of months now and I'm still waiting for the exciting stuff. That's the problem with being 6 . . . I am ready to do all the fun and exciting things and everyone just keeps telling me to practice, practice, practice . . . BORING!!!!

I am trying my best to keep a positive attitude . . . hopefully this New Year will be filled with many improvements. I already told Mommy that I am going to do my best in school. Maybe we can get things back to normal around here, because I really need a vacation.

I hope you all had a much better year than I and wish you a very Merry Christmas and a truly Happy New Year!!!

Love, Christian

RELIGION

The World Book Encyclopedia says that religion is "man's acceptance of the existence of supreme and super-human powers, usually inherent in beings or gods who are worshipped by the believers. Systems ordinarily acquire ceremonial rites and practices which are strictly adhered to."

Too much has been written about religion to collect or summarize, but I believe that the Ten Commandments would suffice for a start. Amen.

"The Sawdust Trail" was the name for the old time re-ligious tent meetings, usually held outdoors. On the floor was strewn some sawdust. These tents accommodated a large number of people. There were no loudspeakers, so the pastor usually had an operatic voice.

The good preacher would walk up and down the aisle, gesturing and looking for lost souls. He often mentioned that if we did not reform, we would go straight to hell. Most people who entered the tent had never encountered such a show.

While the gathering would sing a hymn, the preacher beckoned the sinners to walk up the sawdust trail and meet the Lord and be saved. Quite a few came up the trail, and when leaving, they were overjoyed to have been saved. Amen.

When we speak of Billy Graham, and read or watch him on TV or other media messages, we know that he has a word for not only us but for the rest of the world. For those who do not have religious beliefs, there is something to attain to renew their beliefs. He does not want people to stand with a group on top of a hill and be lifted into the heavens to the distant land called heaven.

And don't forget the Salvation Army—good as it can be. They give their services in all disasters. Give a little, receive a lot.

As a scout master for some 60 years and still active, I noticed that any boy from a church background was easier to deal with. They were always more attentive than the rest of the group. They learned the lessons more quickly.

And devout people live longer, too. Research shows that people who go to church are healthier than those who don't. Researchers took blood samples from 1,700 senior citizens and asked them about their church attendance. People who went to church at least once a week had stronger immune systems than the people who rarely went.

We should be thankful that religion has been established as a dominant approach to true beliefs.

A Smart Priest

When I was about twelve, the Forstmann Co. had some thirty homes built, where we kids had a ball. There was a ball field and in back of the property was a swamp that had about a foot of water when it rained. Here we played with a makeshift wooden boat that lasted about an hour before flooding. We stood out of the water, turned over the boat, and sailed on in style.

We had a gang, all around twelve years of age, better known as the gathering of the brains. 'Twas like a football huddle. Here great decisions were made. Little Joey Feist told us about the interesting event that had transpired at his class in the Catholic church school. A nun in his class prepared the students for the proper protocol when a priest visited to review the class. He would be certain to ask some questions about our surrounding world.

The father entered the room and all the students stood up and were quite tense. He asked the first question: Who created the heavens? Came the answer, "God, God, God." Very good, a splendid answer. Next, "Who created our world?" Again, "God, God, God." Smart answer. The last question was, "Who built this church?" Our hero Joey said, in a shaky voice just above a whisper, "The carpenters."

The class was dumbfounded; they were sure Joey would be excommunicated. But to their continued shock, the priest went over to Joey and placed his hands on the boy's head. "My true and faithful servant, you exemplified the true nature of our Christian Catholic beliefs." The nun was amazed.

At our next meeting of the "think tank," Joey explained that, since the class was still confused, he did not know whether he would ever recover from that onslaught. So be it. Amen, and glory be to God.

BIBLEOLOGY

Into our hemisphere the mirage of Adam, from outer space, these two were not ale-e-ins, cause they did not drink. However, I did see an alien, it was in the brewery. He was the alien in charge of brewing.

The story goes that there was Adam, Eve, a snake, and an apple with presence of a worm. I have made a study of numerous persons in the Good Book, and learned how we obtained the valuable material called sugar. Answer: Able raised cane.

Regarding the three wise men, although they never went to college they left a sign on us which was wise guys, wisecrackers, the wise owl, nocturnal bird of prey.

Unfortunately, the women who could not take orders turned to salt. This was tricky. Anyway, she produced salt, which we call the salt of the earth. Samson had a terrific hair cut. She sneaked up on him and—wham!—off goes the hair. Hair ye, hair ye. This story is neither hair nor dare.

My lawyer, a brilliant man, still believes that "affidavit" is a legal term. No way—it's biblical. Affa-David came Goliath.

My dear readers, I will not be struck by lightning for these enlightenments, because as a young lad we went to church on Wednesday for a prayer meeting and Sunday morning to Sunday school, and last but not least church services in the evening.

HOW DO U-LIKA-DAT?

On Sunday nights at eleven on Channel 3, a minister gives a great sermon for a half hour. He first relaxes his group with a little amusement:

The taxi driver and the minister were at the pearly gates. The taxi driver was given much attention, while the minister got very little. He fumed, "Why do I receive so little service?" Pete said, "Cool off, and remember that while you preach, many fall asleep, but when people enter his cab, they begin to pray."

Here's another. A little girl in Sunday school was drawing a picture. The minister bent over and asked here what she was drawing. She said it was a picture of God. The minister smiled and said, "Young lady, nobody knows how God looks." She smiled and said, "When I finish this picture, everyone will know."

THE POPE SLEPT HERE

In his travels to many countries conveying good deeds and good will, I am sure Pope John Paul II remembers the time he spent at the ranch house in Clifton, New Jersey, the home of Dr. Philipzack. I speak of this proudly, because this is the house that I built.

That was before the Cardinal's jet took off to Rome, where he became the great Pope of Rome and a saint beloved by the entire world. Before I jettison the jet to Rome, I will relate the interesting drama of this story. To make this story a little more interesting, let me relate the entire process from purchasing a lot from Myron T. Holman, Sr., who is now president of the Shotmeyer Oil Co.

Since the street called Fenlon Boulevard was a "paper street," after purchasing the property I inquired regarding the existence of a sewer line. It did exist, and the next move was to clear all the unnecessary shrubs and debris from the entrance at Passaic Avenue. With the city's permission, my brother-in-law, Ted Gambuti, cut a temporary road several hundred feet long to access the area in which I would build the ranch house. Incidentally, the sewer line had not been used. When I found it under several inches and after removing the sewer cover there was only some sand, indicating that it was never used and free of any sediment. Ted also put a sewer line to the ranch house. Then began breathtaking hard work for more than a year, because I built almost all of the house by myself, with minimal help. The entire three sides of the house were built with cinder blocks, but the front was brick and wood. The electrical work, plumbing, and heating were done by professionals. The bank loan required that I own the property, and required several stages of building to complete the loan.

I was a quality control supervisor at the Forstmann Woolen Company of Garfield, N.J. It was after work that I was able to work on the ranch house. Years later I sold the ranch house to Dr. Philipzak. (I next built a split-level house next to the ranch house. However, I also sold this house and moved to a nearby area.)

To continue this romantic episode, Dr. Philipzak's wife was an opera singer with a beautiful voice that could be heard throughout the neighborhood. His wife was also the cardinal's niece. The cardinal enjoyed visiting with the Philipzaks. He could be seen swimming in their backyard pool. On occasion, the media would take pictures of the cardinal and publish or televise them

The cardinal never rested. His mystic powers were relegated to any area where he could exercise his good will and blessings. On one of his walks in the neighborhood, he came upon a man busy on his property, hard at work removing some heavy rocks. "My good man," he said, "it is very admirable to do hard work, but life is too short to work so hard." Joe was astounded, and promised to mend his ways. The cardinal then blessed him and went on his way.

It is of great interest to view the pope on TV and follow his great contributions to the world. May Pope John Paul II live forever in body and soul.

Pete S. and wife Irene are strong Catholics and travel great distances just to see and hear him. It was at one of these sessions that the pope arrived with his entourage and was ready to exit the car but there was a hard rain. The pope stepped out of the car and as if by magic the rain stopped. The program was in full force and again the pope was ready to depart and was ready to enter the car and by gosh it stopped raining.

THE OLD CHURCH

As very young children we attended a storefront church. After several years, the heads of the church decided to construct a real church. The First Hungarian Baptist Church was located on Monroe Street in Garfield, adjacent to the chemical company. The church is still standing, but it is now the Albanian American Islamic Center.

In that little church I recall that people were baptized on the stage. They had an area that was filled with water, and the minister told the person to clasp hands, and he was then dunked backwards down into the water. We had a membership of about 130 people, and I was the only one that never got baptized, because I told the minister that if needed a bath, I would take it at home. People were horrified.

The Kurtz family sang in the choir, acted in plays, and had a small band.

When young people were ready to marry, the minister performed the ceremony, after which the couple was presented with a free dinner in the main hall of the church. Then they were given money and sent on their way.

The church was very active. The Men's Club and Women's Club were very valuable to the church, as well as the Young People's group, the choir, and a small band. Prayer sessions were held on Wednesday evenings, services were held on both Sunday morning and Sunday evening, with Sunday school in the afternoon.

We also formed a cadet corps consisting of young members. We called it the Christian Brotherhood Club, or C.B. Club. Our cadet club decided to take a trip to the mountains and after inquiring about a place to camp we became acquainted with a surgeon by the name of Dr. Fink. Knowing our background, he permitted us to camp in the area of his beautiful home. At the base of our camp we erected our tents. There was a little old footbridge under which ran a swift running brook. Joseph Palkovich, our fearless leader, formed an expedition with the aid of one of the boys to purchase provisions in town. On the way back his assistant, too young to drive, asked permission to try his luck at the wheel. Along this country road he lost control and the Ford slid off the road and ran into a pole. This old

Ford was built really solid, and there was no damage. The supplies were located on the front seat. Among the purchases were two pounds of bologna. Because of the impact of the car, out flew all the baloney onto the ground. We reluctantly retrieved the mess. Back at the camp, being of sound mind, I proposed a lineup along the stream. Each boy washed the slices and passed them to the next washer. Finally, at suppertime, the bits of sand that remained gave us (as John Wayne would say) "true grit."

While the doctor stood on his porch, Joe blew taps on his bugle at the evening campfire. The doctor would stand at attention on his porch and salute us.

A railroad track runs on the street in front of the church. Trains would come over the Passaic River and pass right in front of the church. Although members of the church got used to the trains, eventually they laid new tracks and built a new bridge over the river.

Trains still run on the old track along Monroe Street. One of the local fellows says that a man on the train wears a cowboy hat and boots, and that this character has done that for twenty years.

The little church that is 100 years old plays an important part in the lives and stories of many people.

John and Mary Tarr died at a young age, leaving their six children without any help. Along came the church people, and some were adopted and changed their names.

ARNOLD TARR

Arnold Tarr lived with us after his parents died. In 1930, he decided to strike out on his own. He was hitchhiking through Lincolnton, North Carolina, when the driver of the car offered him a job. He got involved with the high school boxing team, and was the Carolinas Golden Gloves middleweight champion from 1934 to 1936. His nickname was "Jersey." Arnold married in 1937 and spent 18 months at Pearl Harbor in 1942-43 as a civilian with the Navy Department. In 1943 he enlisted in Army and served in Italy and Austria, as well as serving with the Russians for six months in 1945. As a member of local guard unit he went to Korea 50-52 (where, he says, "we froze our asses off"). He spent 30 years as a police officer, and 20 years as Chief of Police of Lincolnton. He has two daughters, six grandchildren, and twelve great grandchildren.

BILL COOKE

Another Tarr brother was Bill Cooke, who was very loyal to his father and mother. He told me the story about how his father loved chicken soup, so he made a pot of soup for him and his father said it was great. "What do you call this soup?" he asked, and Bill said that it was called miracle soup. Dad asked why, and Bill said "It's a miracle if you find the chicken."

Bill is a great adventurer, who loves hunting and fishing and his family. He and his wife, Jackie, have two sons, Carmine and John.

Bill worked at the 9-11 World Trade Center site (see the wonderful photos in Chapter Two). He is an Army veteran who retired from the Clifton, New Jersey, police department after 30 years of service, including 11 years in the tactical street crime unit, three years in the motorcycle division, and 12 years as a detective. Recently he worked on the tactical response team, where he participated in hostage rescue, high risk warrant service, and barricade subject arrests.

Bill and his friend cut out crosses from the 9-11 steel structure, which they distributed to people who were involved in the rescue effort.

A PIECE of HISTORY
TRAGEDY of SEPTEMBER 11, 2001
This cross was made from the remains
of a steel beam retrieved from
The World Trade Center.

Acquired by: Bill Cooke
Crafted by: Mike Donetz
Courtesy of: Affinito Machine, LLC
Herald News 9/5/02

DOCTORS

THE EYES HAVE IT

During my basic training at Camp Crowder, Mo., a routine physical turned up a small growth in my left eye. My next appointment was at the army base hospital. The operating major, an interesting fellow, wanted to put me at ease. Well, soldier, what has caused this plight? With malice towards none, I was very pleased to see that the army permitted me to express myself. "Well, sir, this one evening as I attended a movie, I had my eye on a fellow's seat, and he sat on it."

After my overseas duty, the war being over, I returned to the good old USA. The next problem was to obtain an implant in my left eye, the same old eye. Incidentally, the right eye also had an implant, but to this day has given no trouble. Back again to the left eye, for some undetermined reason it gave me a serious problem. I seemed to have lost my sight, for I could only view about less than half an inch. My doctor rushed me to a specialist who had to tie up the nerve endings. I spent nine days there in the hospital. Back at the ranch, this left eye now had a vision of about 60%.

With a drum roll, we move into the realm of eye-dol-ogy, forsooth.

As a house painter, one day I was sweeping off a garage roof when all of a sudden the broom came up out of nowhere and hit me square in the eye. Yes, my endangered species, suddenly it was the same old eye as it used to be! Naturally, I closed up shop and sauntered over to the eye man. What gives? I queried. He stroked his beard, tottered a little, and said, "Man, when the broom hit you in the eye, it moved away from the pan area, readjusted its position, and a better focus predominated." At this moment, I was under the impression that I would be highlighted in the science magazine and become a celebrity.

I was beside myself (what the hell does that mean?). Before the incident, my left eye had a sight of about 70%. but now the vision improved to about 90%. Also, before, if I touched the eye it was painful, but not anymore. Another plus for me was that when I viewed a face it no longer seemed a little blurred. It was very distinct.

After the exam, I suggested that the doctor set up a sign reading, Broom Aid.

The eye is a terrible thing to destroy. Some wise men say, A penny before the eye can blot out the light of day. I say, Two pennies before each eye can make you blind.

Here's a tribute to the doctors who take such good care of my sister Mitzie and me.

Let's start with Dr Joseph Porter. He's tough, considerate, efficient and smiling. He has Johnny, who swings a mean stethoscope. We fondly call him Doc Watson (no relation to Holmes).

Then there's Dr. Michael F. Ardito, who is congenial and liked by staff and public alike.

My vet, David G. Staubach, asked how my cat got the name Flash. I told him that at the time, at night, there were lights flashing in the sky above New York City, according to the television. I decided to go in the back yard to view them. At that moment, a small figure was barely visible in the shadows. The next morning, there was the cat. So I called him Flash.

Let's sneak my foot doctor in with the others. He is Dr. Martin Conserva. He comes from a large family. His father was a barber, and cut hair for all the big shots in the Forstmann Woolen Co. Dr. Martin's motto is "Put your best foot forward—but treat both of them." As many times he has treated me and Mitz, I always have to foot the bill.

FAMILY

OUR MOTHER—QUITE A LADY

MY WIFE HELEN

When I was first courting my wife Helen, we went with her mother to visit her relatives in West Virginia. This was in a high mountainous area, and there was a large coal mine, of which Helen's father was the superintendent. To get to the top of the mountain was a winding dirt road, but the young boys would ride down, some sitting on the hood of the car. Fearless.

So now was the time to meet her kin. Her uncles had big jobs there, a tough group. With a hard handshake, one of her uncles suggested that I take a ride deep down the mine shaft. This was not the usual way to enter a mine, but they would test me, a city slicker. Well, little did they know that a scoutmaster who led his scout troop through snake-infested country would not fear a little mine-sweeping.

The go-cart was a flat car that could hold two men, so they sat me down and laid me back so that I could fit into a small hole in the earth. Oh, joy. We went down through hell, at high speed. Don't sit up: maintain your head. Finally they noticed that yours truly didn't need any nose powdering.

Helen's father passed away from "black lung." I later made arrangements so that her mother could collect from the government for it.

MY SON PAUL AND HIS MOTHER, 1943

PAUL AND HIS WIFE EZZIE

TRUE LOVE

Paul's hobby is a steam engine train that required several years to build. He is also a member of a club in South Jersey that has a fabulous set of tracks, with gates and colorful scenery. He owns a few antique cars that have brought him some trophies and ribbons

Paul also has a 30-foot Morgan sailboat. One day he and Ezzie went too far out and were greeted by a storm. Essie was blown overboard. She was wearing a lifejacket and had no trouble maintaining her position, and Paul immediately turned the boat around and saved his wife. The day's ordeal over, they went back to the wharf and dragged their luggage up to the car.

Paul embraced Ezzie and said, "Boy, we really had fun!" She nodded her head. At first I thought it was the flies that did it, but then I realized she was trying to agree with him.

My Sister Mitzie

Mitzie turned 95 in 2004. People hear that and say, "God bless her." I would say he did.

RON TUMA

Mitzie's nephew Ronald F. Tuma, PhD, is Senior Associate Dean for Research and Chair of the Department of Physiology at Temple University School of Medicine. As a researcher studying stroke and multiple sclerosis, he has published many books and papers. His teaching has won numerous awards.

LOUIS J. KURTZ

My brother, the Rev. Jouis J. Kurtz, built a home in New Brunswick, N.J., then built the same kind of home in Palm Bay, Florida and helped build a church nearby. He was the administrator of the Hungarian Baptist Church. The town wanted him to become mayor.

CHARLES KURTZ

My brother Charles, the eldest in the family, was in line for the vice presidency of Forstmann Woolen Co. He was interested in photography, and sang in the church choir.

MY SISTER ROSALIE (LIBBY) MARRIED MYRON HOLMAN,
WHO IS NOW THE PRESIDENT OF SHOTMEYER OIL CO.

THE MIDAS TOUCH

This story involves Myron Holman and me, at the United States Signal Corps in Camp Crowder, Missouri.

I, Edward Kurtz, of normal health, was in charge of a barracks with about forty men. This one day, at the mess hall, I saw Myron at the table. He was a recruit in basic training. We immediately became friends.

"Hey, kid," I said, "let's go to the movies," which were in camp. Some time later, I asked him to go out of town so that he could meet some of my friends in towns nearby. We attended some of the local church affairs, where I lectured about the great need for Scouting, and how it would help young men to adjust to daily problems as well as to learn confidence.

I taught a class of slow speed code at five words a minute. Next they sent me to a high speed code class of 25 words a minute. Guess who was the instructor. Yes, Myron Holman.

My sister Libby decided to visit me on the post. Naturally, she met the good-looking Myron, and thus began my prediction of a fierce adventure. She met Mr. Larsen, the movie owner, and various others, which gave her and Myron an attitude to become fast friends. Time motivates. They finally decided to get married. Our dear friend Mr. Larsen decided to give them a wedding present and supplied the wedding feast as well as any other monetary inclusions.

First let's talk about the "Midas Touch." A common figure of speech, I remember the story which was presented to the class. They said it was associated with the story of the mythical king. When a person is successful in whatever he undertakes, we say that he has the "Midas Touch."

Midas Touch—Myron Touch

Myron stayed on to teach code for about a year while I was assigned to a company of specialists that was shipped to England. Finally, he was flown to Germany and we kept in touch.

The war over, Myron, my sister, and Myron Jr. (no middle name) moved into our house. At the time I worked at the Forstmann Woolen Company, and I obtained a job for Myron. Myron Jr., was about seven and was loved by my sister Mitzie. In fact, they had their own "laughing place" in the hall stairway. They would sit there and scream with laughter. (Mitzie and I still use the same place.)

When the Forstmann mills closed, leaving thousands without jobs, Myron applied to the Shotmeyer Gasoline Co., while I sent my resumes to about fifteen plants. No luck—they said I was great in textile but not qualified in their companies' products. Next move, I went into the house painting business.

But the Myron Touch rides again. Year after year, Myron was promoted at Shotmeyer from common clerk to his current position as President. You say, what background did he require for this magnificent position? Reminds me of story about the meeting the president of the company had with the staff where he presented a young man who was then a plain worker. He told them that the young man had risen from the ranks, as foreman, supervisor, manager and now vice president. The young man bowed his head and said, "Thanks, Dad."

Let's muse. Shotmeyer came from Holland with a new pair of wooden shoes, and also worked his way up to being owner of the gas company. He did not like the "fancy pants lawyers" or businessmen around him, so that Myron fitted in the right position, a country boy who lived on a farm and worked in a lumber yard.

Midas Touch? You bet.

MYRON SR. AND MYRON JR.

MYRON JUNIOR IN HIGH SCHOOL

Here's how Myron Jr. describes his life:

I grew up a reasonably normal (and probably very spoiled) kid, what with my folks, my Aunt Sissy, Uncle Ed, and my grandparents all doting on me.

When I was old enough to work, my first job was selling shoes in a local Shoprite (yes, back in the '60s Shoprite was a complete department store!). I worked there through high school and college (Fairleigh Dickinson University, Teaneck Campus—aka Harvard-on-the-Hackensack or "Fairly Ridiculous").

After college I worked in the main office of the company, Meldisco, and worked my way up to Director of

Data Processing (with a staff of 150) by the age of 26. I enjoyed those years a lot.

After 25 years I left Meldisco and joined Dad in the oil business. Then, in 1989, I left the oil biz and formed my own company, dealt in real estate transactions, made some investments, and started a remodeling company. And to this day, I'd like to think I am still making people happy with new family rooms, bathrooms, kitchens . . . and still find time to make some renovations happen to my own properties. I just remodeled and moved into a fabulous townhouse that I built right here in scenic downtown Ramsey, New Jersey.

Just a word about some of my life's passions. I always tried to master individual sports, played a lot of sports over the years, and got pretty good at them: bowling (195 average), tennis (AA player), billiards (played with the big boys), and now golf (hey, I actually shot par 72 twice!)

Life has been good to me. Great experiences, wonderful family, terrific friendships. Not many people can boast as much!

Families fade away, as did mine. Of the five children, only Mitzie and I are here to fend for ourselves.

Let's trim the wick on the kerosene lamp, puff up the pillow, and go to bed. Sweet dreams.

A Tip to the Wise is Fluorescent

Many times a good invention has failed here in the United States because some high-and-mighty decided to ignore it. Now the foreign countries welcome it and the person gets rich. Same with books.

It takes several thousand dollars to enter the invention field, and requires about a year to complete the process. I've gotten help with my inventions from
Vince Kapolka
Advent Product Development
Suite 215
100 Menlo Park
Edison, NJ 08837

Organizing the Confusion

This book has been arranged by the famous Lady Laura, of Silk Purse Editorial Services. She is a PhD.

She arranged my first book, titled *How to Win Friends and Influenza,* as well.

For many months, I tried to get someone to process my writing, but to no avail. I told my nephew Myron Holman, Jr., to call a college. Perhaps they might know someone to edit my book. He did call, and a professor at the college told him to call Laura.

About the Author

Edward Kurtz is a lifelong resident of New Jersey. At 18 he went to work for the Forstmann Woolen Co. in Garfield as an oiler boy, and rose to quality control supervisor. When the mill closed, he formed a house painting business.

During the Second World War he enlisted in the Army Signal Corps, spending one year at Camp Crowder, Mo., and subsequently serving overseas in five countries as an instructor in radio communications. He holds an amateur extra class radio license.

At 21, Ed organized a Cadet Corps of 35 boys in Clifton, and has served the Boy Scouts of America as a scoutmaster since 1940. He has earned the Silver Beaver award and is still active in scouting. He also started a Junior Achievement group in Passaic.

Ed lives in Clifton, New Jersey with his 95-year-old sister, Mitzie.

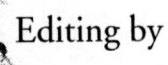Editing by

SILK PURSE EDITORIAL SERVICES
P.O. Box 691
Tuxedo Park, New York 10987
editor@silkpurse.net

Printed in the United States
23637LVS00001B/153-182